An Unexpected
CHRISTMAS

An Unexpected
CHRISTMAS

Inspired by a true story

Denise George

new
hope
PUBLISHERS

Birmingham, Alabama

New Hope® Publishers
P.O. Box 12065
Birmingham, AL 35202-2065
www.newhopepubl.com

Library of Congress Cataloging-in-Publication Data
George, Denise.
An unexpected Christmas / Denise George.
p. cm.
ISBN 1-56309-715-X
I.   Title.
PS3557.E475U54 2003
813'.6—dc21
2003008060

All Scripture quotations, unless otherwise indicated, are taken
from the HOLY BIBLE, NEW INTERNATIONAL VERSION®.
NIV®. Copyright ©1973, 1978, 1984 by International Bible
Society. Used by permission of Zondervan. All rights reserved.

Interior illustrations by Tanna Griggs

ISBN: 1-56309-715-X
N994139 • 1003 • 10M1

*The events of this story are adapted from the experiences of the author.
Names, dates, and details may have been changed.*

For Willene Williams Wyse —
my mother, my lifelong friend —
with much love and heartfelt
appreciation.

The Beginning

"I tell you the truth,
whatever you did for one of
the least of these brothers of mine,
you did for me."

Matthew 25:40

*I*n the center of our family room bookcase rests an old, dirty shoe. It has a large gaping hole in the toe and a sheet of cardboard stuffed in the sole. The shoe has been a treasure of mine for more than twenty years. It is the dearest and most unforgettable Christmas present I've ever received.

I celebrated Christmas that year dripping wet and huddled down in a filthy, dark alley in Chelsea, an inner-city community located near Boston. At the back door of Grady's Diner, I knelt on the ground, dirty, disheveled, and chilled to the bone. As midnight ticked into Christmas Day, a freezing sleet began to pelt the violent inner city....

Chapter 1

I first met Johnny Cornflakes several months before that memorable Christmas Day in a dark, cold alley. That wasn't his real name; no one knew his real name. In fact, no one knew anything about Johnny—who he was or where he came from. The street kids had dubbed the tired old man "Johnny Cornflakes" because Johnny lived on the streets and searched the city's trash bins for the last few remaining flakes left in discarded cereal boxes.

Sometimes Grady, the owner of Grady's "Greasy Spoon" Diner down the street, tossed Johnny crusty tidbits off customer's plates. Grady was a mean old man, used foul language, and kept an unfiltered cigarette dangling from his lips. He often showed the street kids the array of tattoos that covered his arms and chest. Needless to say, I didn't care much for Grady. But Johnny loved him.

My husband, Timothy, and I, native Southerners, had come to the New England area to work and study. Timothy had been accepted at Harvard Divinity School to work on a Master of Divinity degree. He had also found a job in a large, old, run-down church on Shurtleff Street, right in the center of the inner city of Chelsea, Massachusetts. I worked with the city's preschoolers in the church's basement day care. We lived in the church parsonage.

I met Johnny Cornflakes unexpectedly on the night of my first dinner party in Chelsea. I unpacked and polished

9

the silver tea service, a recent wedding gift from my parents and our most valuable possession. I carefully laid each piece of church-owned china in exactly the correct place for each guest. We expected our six out-of-town guests within minutes. I desperately wanted to impress these people.

"Denise, this will be a wonderful dinner party. Everything is perfect. Please, Denise, just relax and enjoy the evening," Timothy urged.

"It's just got to be perfect," I said, as I filled the church's century-old sugar bowl, the last relic that hadn't been stolen.

"I want this dinner party to be perfect."

I made one last glance at the table. The table was old but fairly steady. But the chairs—I worried about the chairs. They had been repaired too many times, and they seemed too wobbly to be safe. The table looked nice draped in a lace cloth. Our silver tea service sparkled under the candlelight. And I figured that if the guests sat down gently, the chairs would hold. We could afford only onion soup, baked beans, and "sweet potato surprise," but the elegance of the silver tea service more than compensated for the simple meal.

"Come in," I heard Timothy say as he opened the front door and welcomed our distinguished guests.

I took a deep breath, smoothed my long velvet skirt, and followed Timothy to the door.

"Just relax, Denise," Timothy once again whispered in my ear as he seated the final guest at the table.

So far, so good, I thought. I turned to Timothy. "I just want our guests to remember this dinner party for a long time," I said under my breath and furrowed my brow to show him I meant business. We would soon find out that Timothy had forgotten to padlock the front door.

Well, thanks to a certain Johnny Cornflakes, our guests would indeed remember this dinner party for a long time! As I stood to serve the soup, the front door flew open. And there, in all of his inebriated glory, stood Johnny Cornflakes. With a gentleman's bow and a toothless grin, he limped toward the table. The guests gasped. I was too startled to move. Unashamedly, Johnny picked up the large serving spoon and began shoveling my "sweet potato surprise" into his mouth. At the sight, my dark eyes widened and my mouth flew open.

Timothy seemed unalarmed. He gently took Johnny's arm and led him to the kitchen. From the pots still hot on the stove, Timothy heaped a china plate full of food and gave it to Johnny, who sat at the kitchen table and relished his unexpected dinner.

When Timothy returned, I still stood wide-eyed and open-mouthed with the soup ladle rattling in my hand.

My proper southern upbringing never included this type of social dilemma.

"What should I do now?" I mumbled to myself. Our

dignified guests were also speechless. No one knew what to say.

"Well, let's eat," Timothy said cheerfully as he walked into the dining room. He acted like nothing out of the ordinary had happened. I quickly served the soup, but my hands shook and I felt rattled down to my golden-slippered toes. Trying to remain calm, I moved gracefully back to my chair. I slightly lifted my long velvet skirt to sit down, but as I came down, another nightmare took place. I felt the old chair leg give way. I was in mid-air and falling, and there was nothing I could do to keep my balance. I hit the dining room floor hard. The jolt knocked the breath out of me.

Out of the corner of one eye, I saw our dinner guests gasp and jump from their seats to help me. My legs were pointed to the ceiling like a "V," and my long velvet skirt settled somewhere up around my waist. During those embarrassing moments, only one thought came to mind: *If only my mother could see me now!*

The racket was loud enough to bring Johnny Cornflakes staggering out of the kitchen. Before my guests could reach me, Johnny had both his food-covered hands around my waist and was tugging with all his might to lift me from my place on the floor.

"Get away from me! Get away from me!" I shouted at Johnny. "This is all your fault! Just get away!" But Johnny would not be deterred. We had shared a feast with him that night, and he was determined to come to my rescue.

He somehow managed to lift me halfway to my feet, but in the chaos, fell and pulled me down with him. In front of our distinguished guests, Johnny and I lay sprawled on the dining room floor.

"Timothy!" I shouted. "Help me, Timothy!"

What happened at that point made Laurel and Hardy look like international dignitaries. My dinner party became a side show, complete with flying food and slapstick comedy. By the time Johnny finally let loose of my middle, my blouse hung out of my skirt, my hose were snagged, one earring was missing, and my dignity was destroyed. My guests wrapped their hands around their entire faces trying to stifle their horror and their laughter.

When Timothy unintentionally let out a tiny muffled laugh, I stormed from the room.

"This is not funny, Timothy!" I screamed from the stairs.

Timothy followed me upstairs while our guests sat quietly downstairs, gazing at the uneaten food on the table. Johnny Cornflakes sat down in Timothy's chair and "entertained" our guests in our absence. He also finished off my "sweet potato surprise."

"Well, Timothy, I hope you are amused," I said hotly. "That old drunk has ruined my dinner party! I hate that old man! Just get him out of my house and out of my life. Now! I never want to see Johnny Cornflakes again."

Chapter 2

*S*everal weeks before that disastrous dinner party, we as newlyweds had traveled to Chelsea, a journey that took us many miles from our southern birthplace. At that time, at the tender age of 21, I was in no way emotionally prepared to embark upon the journey Timothy had planned. It would prove a life-changing trek into the unknown.

We spent our last August night in the South with my parents in Rossville, Georgia. We packed the old green Plymouth Satellite with everything we owned—typewriter, sewing machine, a few dishes, the silver tea service, and the beautiful quilt my grandmother's sister, Aunt Gertrude, had painstakingly stitched for us. Before we climbed into bed late that night, we said our good-nights, and our good-byes; early morning farewells would've been too difficult. At 4:30 A.M. we slipped into the old car and began the trip that would change our lives.

Three days later, we arrived in the New England area. It seemed the end of the earth. We had never been so far away from home. It was another world, another culture. Culture shock set in quickly when we visited our first New England grocery store.

"Where are the grits?" we politely asked the grocer.

He scratched his head, thought a moment, and barked out, "Foreign food section."

And we found them there!

We moved into the crudely furnished church parsonage in Chelsea and immediately began our work.

We had never seen a city like Chelsea before. Some thirty thousand people crowded into Chelsea's confining city limits. People packed into wooden apartment buildings like baked beans in a small jar. It was not unusual to find a twelve-member family living in a two-room top floor apartment. Chelsea residents had little room to move and little space to breathe. I found Chelsea so different from the vast, green forests and rich farmland I knew and loved.

Chelsea's children came in all colors, shapes, and sizes. They spoke dialects I had never heard. Outside, there were few trees to climb, few yards to play in, few streets not congested by traffic, and little money to leave Chelsea in search of greener pastures. The children roamed the dirty streets to escape the boredom and loneliness of crowded apartments.

I'll never forget the day five-year-old David, a small Spanish boy who lived in a foster home, asked me what a flower was. He had never seen a real flower push its way through soil and bloom. Chelsea had no flowers and little soil in the city to grow them. It was not unusual for a child to live his entire life in Chelsea, grow up, raise a family, and never see the flower gardens of the world.

Johnny Cornflakes was the first alcoholic I had ever

met. He slept under apartment porches, roamed the dirty streets looking for "valuable" garbage, and occasionally ate the leftovers that Grady and other local restaurant owners tossed out to him. As far as Johnny Cornflakes was concerned, Grady served up a king's banquet back there in the dirty alley behind the diner. Chelsea proved to be a new experience for me.

Growing up in the suburban South, I never in my wildest dreams imagined that a city like Chelsea existed anywhere in the United States. I had grown up in a goldfish bowl, in a 1950s traditional southern family—protected, sheltered, and spoiled. Surrounded by acres of large hickory nut trees, green grass, and rose gardens, I basked in nature's beauty. I spent the winters in my comfortable subdivision and the summers on my grandparents' farm. I always had lots of room to roam, trees to climb, roses to smell, and leisure hours to sit in neatly-mowed grass and dream the dreams that young girls dream. Little did I know that within the next few years my life would be turned upside down and inside out, and all my familiar boundaries would be forever erased.

I once heard a resident describe Chelsea as the "armpit" of the United States. In my opinion, it deserved the name. It was a terrible place to live and work and raise a family. Dog droppings covered the streets, and the strong scent of old alcohol, vomit, and urine rose from the sidewalks. On hot, windless days, the smell proved unbearable.

Nothing green grew in Chelsea. The concrete city was never quiet, and the cacophony of sirens from fire engines and police cars never ceased morning or night. Chelsea also proved to be a rather dangerous firetrap. Old wooden apartment buildings, badly in need of repair, were stacked together like decks of playing cards. Oil furnaces often caught fire and exploded, sending buildings up in flames. Since corruption ruled the city, fire and building codes had become relaxed. Chelsea had had a major fire the century before, but the blazing tragedy had long been forgotten. Because Chelsea was located next to Boston's airport, Boeing 747s routinely descended so low over Chelsea that I could wave to the passengers.

I remember no scenery in Chelsea, and the windows of the parsonage looked directly into the windows of the apartment dwellers on all sides. To put it frankly, I thought Chelsea was a major eyesore—truly the "armpit" of the United States!

Sunday morning smells were perhaps the worst of all. Saturday night in Chelsea was "party night" for the vagrant teenagers who roamed the streets, drained bottles of cheap whiskey, and slept in dark alleyways. On Saturday nights, I often lay in bed and listened to the sounds of empty bottles breaking against concrete sidewalks.

Saturday nights also brought out the street gangs and unspeakable violence. Violence had almost destroyed the city. With the necessity of padlocks and window bars, community members had become prisoners in their own homes trying to protect themselves and their children against senseless violence. Knife fights on our front stoop were commonplace. Fortunately, during those years not too many gang members carried guns, but knives and fists proved just as deadly. Rival gangs routinely left their unfortunate victims lying in the streets to be discovered on Sunday mornings. Discarded drug needles, broken bottles, and human waste in the streets made Sunday mornings a major clean-up time for the church's front-stairs crew before the handful of Chelsea church-goers ascended the steep sanctuary steps.

The contrast between Saturday night and Sunday morning bewildered me. Singing hymns and reciting litanies seemed to somehow redeem the reveries of the previous night. When on Sunday mornings the Chelsea church lit the one bright light in the whole community, the few who saw the light and sensed its warmth gathered like moths around its flame. The church was a candle in a community of darkness.

Our elderly church members, like old Mrs. Bena, a kind, loving woman and a lifelong Chelsea resident, still remembered Chelsea as a place of high society, classical concerts, and Sunday afternoon strolls. More than a hundred years before, the grand old church had been painstakingly built from hand-cut rock and boasted elegant stained glass windows and a tall cross-shaped steeple.

In fact, Mrs. Bena's father had helped build the church. But through the years, something had happened to the city. The decay spread year after year until, more than a century later, Chelsea had become home for the not so rich and famous, but the down-and-outers, transients, homeless elderly, and hopeless teenagers. "Abandon hope, all ye who enter here," seemed to be Chelsea's unspoken motto.

In that hostile setting Timothy and I lived, worked, loved, and learned. For a southern girl, Chelsea proved a tremendous shock. I didn't even unpack my dishes for a while. I didn't want to stay. I lay in bed at night and dreamed of going back home where "decent" people lived and order ruled. During those first few months, I felt miserable, homesick, and afraid—often with good reason.

Chapter 3

*I*n order to attract Chelsea's young people to the church, Timothy started an open-door "coffee house" on Friday nights in the church basement. He offered music, games, soft drinks, and potato chips. Mrs. Bena often added homemade sugar cookies to our menu. That usually proved enough encouragement to bring in transient and troubled teens. When the potato chips and sugar cookies ran out, Timothy invited the teens to a brief Bible study.

We had a small core of "regulars" who came faithfully every Friday night. Most had had tragic pasts, but through his study, each was finding a new faith in a loving God. Their lives were taking on new meaning and new exuberance.

They were a most unusual group of people. Weird might be a better word to describe them. Lisa and Jenny, for instance, had run away from troubled homes as young teens. Rick had been addicted to heroin and various other illegal drugs. Sam grew up in an abusive foster home, ran away at age 14, and ended up in prison for theft. Jason had been a gang member. Paul had been mixed up with a drug dealer. We found him lying on the church steps one Sunday morning, unconscious and badly beaten.

These teens came to form a tight-knit group; they supported and encouraged each other. They shared clothes and food and helped each other find places to live. They were each different from the other, yet they had so much in common. They had known street life and had learned to fight and survive in a hostile environment. They were tough kids who wore torn jeans, oversized t-shirts, and army surplus combat boots. They wore their hair long and their clothes tattered. They had no money, but they enjoyed a mysterious type of joy that I had yet to discover.

Timothy fit in nicely with Chelsea's young people. He left his "clean-cut" look back in Georgia and let his light brown hair grow past his ears and spill onto his collar. He also stopped shaving and allowed a bushy beard to take over his face. The first day we arrived in Chelsea, he donned overalls and boots, rolled up his shirt sleeves, and went to work. The teens loved Timothy and claimed him as one of their own.

I, however, chose to bring my southern culture with me to Chelsea. No way would I wear overalls and boots; I stuck to my bounces and flounces and bows in my hair. I definitely did not "fit in."

Nor did I want to.

It was on a rather unremarkable Friday night that I again encountered Johnny Cornflakes. Our little group of faithful "regulars" met as usual in the church basement for Bible study. We formed a small circle with metal folding chairs, opened our Bibles, and began our study.

"Sam," Timothy asked. "Would you please read from Matthew 25?" Sam fumbled through his Bible. He had never read Matthew before and had no idea where the book was located in the Bible.

"It's in the New Testament, the first book," Timothy gently helped him. I sighed a loud breath of pure impatience as I waited for Sam to find what I considered the easiest book in the Bible to find. For a full five minutes, Sam thumbed through his Bible trying to locate the Gospel of Matthew. He began to read, slowly and carefully, one word at a time. He stopped from time to time and looked up at Timothy. Timothy nodded his encouragement, a sort of, *You're doing great, Sam,* and Sam continued to read. Sam had long before dropped out of school and simple reading proved difficult for him. But his zeal and enthusiasm for his newfound faith more than made up for his lack of reading skills.

I knew the passage in Matthew 25 forwards and backwards. In fact, I knew it so well that it held little meaning for me anymore. While Sam read, my thoughts drifted back to my grandparents' farm and Inky the pony, Little Man the dog, and the afternoon watermelon slicings for the grandchildren.

It took a long time, but Sam continued to read. "For I was hungry and you gave me something to eat, I was thirsty and you gave me something to drink, I was a stranger and you invited me in, I needed clothes and you clothed me, I was sick and you looked after me, I was in prison and you came to visit me."

Sam stopped reading. His face turned crimson as he lifted his young tired eyes and looked into the faces of those sitting around him, those who had known hunger and thirst, who had been sick and addicted, who had needed clothes, who had been unwanted strangers, who had been in prison.

He wiped his eyes with his sleeve, and after a long moment, he continued reading. "Lord, when did we see you hungry and feed you, or thirsty and give you something to drink? When did we see you a stranger and invite you in, or needing clothes and clothe you? When did we see you sick or in prison and go to visit you?"

"I tell you the truth," Sam continued reading, "whatever you did for one of the least of these brothers of mine, you did for me." The little group sat very still and quiet after Sam stopped reading. Most had not heard these words before and they had much to ponder. They knew firsthand what it meant to be hungry, naked, sick, and imprisoned. The expressions on their faces showed they needed some time to digest what Sam had just read to them.

For a long time the group of teenagers talked with Timothy about the meaning of "the least of these," and our responsibility to those who are needy, to those we call "neighbor." I must admit that while the group pondered the Scriptures, I allowed my thoughts to continue to drift 1,200 miles away. *Oh, I miss home so much,* I inwardly moaned. *Why did we ever leave Georgia to come to this god-forsaken place? How I hate this city with its dirt and its crime and its disgusting people.*

Before I could continue my inward complaining, however, the basement door burst open. A cold October wind blasted the room, wildly flipping Bible pages.

Johnny Cornflakes staggered inside. He wore a navy blue suit, twenty years out of style and covered with city dirt. Wisps of white hair danced around his face—a face carved by years of hard drinking and hostile New England winters.

With stooped shoulders and an age-etched frown, he resembled a Ringling Brother's circus clown as he limped into the room. He proceeded to step on eight pairs of feet only to land, amazingly, upright in the chair next to mine. Once seated, he turned his entire body toward me and with large bloodshot eyes gazed into my face.

Still staring at me, Johnny opened his food-encrusted, toothless mouth and smiled. The stench of body odor and alcohol hit me full force. I jerked my head away and wrapped my hand tightly over my face. My stomach reeled. I thought I would be sick.

"Excuse me," I said, jumping up, my hand still tightly wrapped around my mouth, and headed for the ladies room down the hall. For a full ten minutes, I hung my head over the sink, breathed deeply, and struggled to keep back the nausea.

When I reentered the room and sat down in my chair, I longed with every part of my being to be back home with the people I knew and loved. I felt large hot tears run along the rims of my eyelids.

How I intensely disliked this place. How I intensely disliked the old man who sat beside me in the worn-out suit, who smelled bad, and who staggered his way through life.

As I sat in the Bible study and eyed Johnny, I thought to myself, *Johnny, isn't it enough that you ruined my dinner, embarrassed me to death, and made my party an evening that my dinner guests will never forget?! Must you now follow me into my church, plop down beside me, and breathe your whiskey breath in my face?*

But here sat Johnny Cornflakes, right next to my chair, intruding on my study of God's Word.

Chapter 4

Vividly remembering the dinner party Johnny had ruined, I sat stiffly in the metal chair while the others sat quietly, still focused on the meaning of Matthew 25. Johnny's body odor was unbearable. When I turned to give him an angry glare, I noticed all eyes were on Johnny's shoe. I saw it too. His twisted mass of unsocked foot, crippled by a childhood disease, was stuffed into an over-sized shoe with a large gaping hole. Johnny had pushed cardboard into the hole, trying to shut out the blustery New England winter.

Jason broke the uncomfortable silence. "You know, it won't be long till winter snow comes," he said. "I think Jesus would want us to buy Johnny another shoe." The others agreed and immediately emptied their pockets. Jason counted out $15.00 worth of dimes, nickels, and quarters.

"This should be enough for a shoe," he guessed. "Let's get Johnny to the foot doctor tomorrow."

I couldn't believe my ears. They were actually going to spend their money on a shoe for Johnny!

"Well, I believe in helping the poor, but aren't there agencies that could give Johnny a shoe?" I asked.

"With all the papers and red tape," Lisa piped in, "it will be next summer before Johnny gets a shoe." At that point, I decided to keep quiet. Money was so scarce in

Chelsea. We, ourselves, could hardly buy groceries. I hadn't had a new pair of shoes in a year. But if they wanted to spend $15.00 on a shoe for Johnny, I would keep my mouth shut.

The next day Timothy and Rick took Johnny to the foot doctor. "Johnny's foot is so badly deformed," the doctor explained, "a new shoe designed to fit him will cost $113.92."

"One hundred thirteen dollars and ninety-two cents? There's no way we can buy that shoe!" I said to Timothy later that evening when he told me the bad news. "Johnny'll just have to live with cardboard in his shoe."

The next Friday night, we told the coffee-house group about the shoe and the money it would cost.

"Since we can't buy the shoe," I suggested, "let's use the money for something else."

But Rick wouldn't hear of it. "Johnny needs that shoe. Anyway," he asked, looking me squarely in the eye, "isn't Johnny one of the 'least of these' that Jesus talks about?"

"But..."

Rick interrupted me. "We'll just have to somehow earn the money for the shoe!"

The next morning, Lisa, Jenny, Rick, Sam, Jason, and Paul hit the streets of Chelsea in search of odd jobs. They picked up trash, moved furniture, and washed windows. It took them six weeks to earn $113.92. And they bought Johnny's shoe.

It was snowing the next Friday night as we admired the new shoe and waited for Johnny. One hour, two hours, three hours crept by. But Johnny didn't come.

"Do you think he's left town?" Paul asked.

"Maybe he's sick somewhere, or even...dead," Jenny said.

I couldn't stand it any longer. "The old drunk!" I blurted out. "He could at least come get his shoe!"

Then Rick spoke. "Well, we'll just have to go out and find Johnny and take the shoe to him."

"It's not safe to be on the streets this time of night," I warned them.

But they were determined. So I decided to tag along. I followed the small group from behind. Because it was wet and dirty, I didn't want to join them in the search. I walked with them and watched them for the next few hours as they crawled under apartment porches, checked out local restaurant alleys, searched the city's trash bins, and combed the filthy streets calling his name.

When the teenagers emerged from the search, they looked worse than I imagined Johnny himself looked. City grime covered their hands, feet, and even their faces, and mud clung to their clothes. They looked a mess. And they still hadn't found Johnny. They finally gave up the search and we all headed back to the church.

Several days passed. We had a treasure in our midst, a treasure worth $113.92. Sam had been entrusted to "keep the shoe" while we searched day after day for Johnny Cornflakes. But after several weeks of calling out his name and searching for him in the city's back alleys, we finally gave up. Week after week, as our little group carried the shoe to each Bible study, hoping Johnny would show up, we lost a little more hope of ever finding him.

Johnny was gone. He had vanished into thin air.

And we were left with an expensive shoe that would fit only Johnny's twisted foot.

Chapter 5

*O*n the last Friday night in November, we wrapped the shoe in tissue paper and placed it back in its box. Sam tied twine tightly around the large white box, put it under his arm, and took it to his home to keep it safe until the group could decide what to do with it.

Timothy had planned an out-of-town trip on the following night. We spent Saturday morning washing clothes, packing, and counting pocket change to meet his travel expenses.

As he always did when he traveled, Timothy left me plenty of safety instructions.

"Lock the doors, Denise, and check the windows to make sure they're locked, too," he said.

I didn't like the idea of spending Saturday night, or any night, alone in the two-story house, but there was nothing I could do about it. We had been in Chelsea long enough to have had everything we owned stolen. Break-in after break-in had robbed us of all our wedding gifts, with the exception of the silver tea service (which I kept well hidden), a new pair of twin bed sheets, and Aunt Gertrude's handmade quilt. Our old manual typewriter was even stolen during one of the many robberies. Fortunately, thieves chose to rob us when we were away from home. Only one time did I enter the back door while a young thief quickly left the house through the front door.

After each incident, we called the police. Often it took two or three calls before the police came. On several occasions the police never came at all. We filed the necessary reports and went back to work, knowing that little would be done to find the crook or to prevent the next break-in.

And the thieves were growing bolder. They now came in through the padlocked front door in broad daylight. They broke windowpanes and made little effort to hide their intended robbery.

"Be careful," Timothy told me as he slipped into his coat, stepped into the deep snow on that cold November morning, and began his trek to the car. "I'll be back tomorrow."

That night, I quickly checked the first- and second-story windows to make sure they were securely locked. I fastened the front door padlock and checked the back door's bolt. All seemed secure enough. But Saturday night was no night to take chances, so I rechecked all the locks before I changed into my nightgown and climbed into bed.

From my bed, I could see out the second story window. It was a clear night. The tall street lamp next to our house showed the streets to be less crowded on this Saturday night. It seemed like some sort of "calm" before the Saturday night "storm." I looked forward to a good night's sleep. Sleep was one way I could escape the horrors of the inner city. When I closed my eyes in sleep, I could be instantly transported anywhere I wanted to go.

I could pretend I was a little girl again back on my grandparents' farm where Mama's lovely flowers bloomed and hickory nut trees grew straight and tall. Their farm had been my summer paradise. Mornings brought gentle rains. Afternoons brought chicken frying in cast-iron skillets, pound cakes cooling on the counter, fried okra, garden corn, and homemade biscuits warming in the oven.

My grandparents never had a lot of money, but Mama always made sure each of her six visiting grandchildren had a dime in hand when the ice cream truck stopped in front of the old white gabled house.

Sleep brought thoughts of Mama and long-ago, faraway memories I thought I had forgotten. As sleep came that late Saturday night, I dreamt about Mama and what I most loved about her. She had a heart of gold. She was a kind and giving woman who loved people and made sure she delivered a big jar of homemade vegetable soup to anyone who fell sick.

I remembered the summer day a little barefoot girl in a torn, dirty dress knocked on her front door. Mama invited her inside. She was about my age, but she didn't look like any of my friends or me. In her small hands, she held some ragged dish towels.

"Would you like to buy some of these?" she asked my grandmother timidly.

Mama smiled, "I sure would. How did you know just exactly what I needed?" Mama went to her secret place where her coins were hidden, and when she returned, I watched her slip a generous handful of coins into the girl's dress pocket.

"I'll buy one dishtowel," she told the girl, "and the rest of the money is for you."

It wasn't long before I felt sleep take over and I gladly relinquished my cherished memories for a needed night's rest. I knew Timothy would arrive very early the next morning to clean the church steps and get everything ready for Sunday's service.

I had become quite accustomed to the routine Saturday night noises. Even though tonight seemed quieter than most Saturday nights, planes still dipped into the neighboring airport, fire engines continued to scream and race up and down Chelsea's narrow streets, and street kids still threw empty bottles against distant city buildings. But those noises didn't usually keep me awake anymore.

Something happened, however, about three o'clock that morning that made me suddenly sit straight up in bed. I turned my head and stopped breathing to listen to the unusual sounds.

Voices. I could hear voices, not loud drunken voices, but voices speaking at a low volume. I slipped out of bed and knelt by the window. Trying not to be seen, I peeked out and saw a sight that made my heart stop.

A dozen or more teenagers stood under my bedroom window. One by one they had climbed over the eight-foot fence and had crept quietly into our yard. Years before, the church custodian had strung sharp barbed wire across the top of the chain link fence to keep the dangerous street kids from climbing it. But the teens jumped over the fence with ease.

In their hands they carried crowbars, making it clear what they intended to do. They didn't see a green Plymouth Satellite in the driveway and assumed no one was home. I knew they planned to break in through a window and rob the house. My mind raced. I had remembered to lock all the windows on the first and second floor. But the garage room window? Had I remembered to lock the garage room window? We used that room for storage. I hadn't been in that part of the house in a long time. Was that window locked? I thought it was, but I couldn't remember.

"Be calm, Denise," I told myself again and again. I made my way across the room to the telephone and dialed the police.

"Officer, please send someone to 27 Bellingham Street! Street kids are breaking into my house!" I cried.

I hung up the receiver and held my breath, hoping the police would hurry. I had no gun, no knife, no protection whatsoever in the house. Up against so many teens, I knew I couldn't defend myself.

"Hurry, please hurry," I cried under my breath and listened for the police car siren. From the window, I watched as they continued to jump over the fence. They had discovered the garage room window. I could hear the scratch of the crowbar as they forced it under the window.

"Hurry!" I cried as I redialed the police. "Please, officer! They are breaking into my window! I'm here by myself! Hurry! Please hurry!"

I knelt back down by the window and silently prayed for God's protection. That's when I heard the window pop. It was locked, but the lock had given way. With others still jumping over the fence, I could hear the sickening sound of the window opening. I waited breathlessly for the police, but heard no siren. I only heard the sound of strong young bodies lifting themselves into the basement through the garage room window. I raced for my bedroom door and firmly fastened the lock. I knew it wouldn't be long now before they found the stairs and bounded up to my bedroom.

Suddenly, I heard a strange voice under my bedroom window call out, "No! You can't go in there!"

I searched the yard. No, it wasn't the police. Again I heard the voice yelling, "Go away! Go away!"

What I heard next sounded like a hard punch to someone's stomach and the sound of gasping and falling. Whoever had been hit was still calling out in a pained voice, "No! You can't go in there!"

In the midst of the heaving and gagging, I heard another loud scream. This was a bone-chilling scream, laced with fear and pain.

"Help me! Help me! I'm hurt!" the young voice cried out.

I peeked out the window and saw one of the teenagers caught in the jagged barbed wire on the top of the eight-foot fence. His knee was torn to the bone and his pants leg was soaked in blood.

Writhing in pain and unable to free himself, he screamed wildly for his buddies. At that moment, the gang of youth inside the house saw their friend hanging from the fence. They turned around and stormed out. Those in the yard also turned and ran to their friend. It took the whole lot of them to untangle his flesh and lift him down.

"He needs a doctor!" someone shouted. One of the teens hot-wired a parked van nearby. They lifted the injured youth into the stolen van, jumped in, and with a loud screech of tires, took off for the nearest hospital.

It took me several minutes to realize what had happened. They were gone—all of them. But I was too afraid to go downstairs. For the longest time, I sat on the floor staring out the window and thanking God for His intervention.

That's when I noticed a shadowy figure emerging from beneath the bedroom window.

"Oh no," I quietly cried and caught my breath. There was still someone down there. I watched the figure as he tried several times to stand up. Heaving, he headed away from the house, his left hand clutching his stomach, his right hand raised to his head.

"Who?" I whispered. "Who are you?"

As the mysterious figure moved toward the street lamp, I noticed a familiar limp.

"Johnny? Could it be you, Johnny?"

Directly under the light, I watched the old man's white wispy hair dance as the cold November winds blew all around him. I also saw one noticeably large shoe print in the snow.

I had quite a story to tell Timothy when he returned later that morning. I still couldn't believe Johnny Cornflakes had been the loud voice I heard, that he had tried to protect me from the gang members, and that he had taken a blow to the stomach on my behalf.

I realized that Johnny's actions did not in the least deter the teens, but he had tried to protect me. I shuddered when I realized the teenagers could have killed the tired old man.

The next Friday night I could hardly wait to tell the others that Johnny Cornflakes was alive, that I had seen him the week before! As we took our places in the cold metal chairs, I recited to them the horrors of the past Saturday night.

"No, the police never came," I answered, as they asked questions all at the same time.

"Yes, I called them a third time, but they still never came."

"Yes, I'm sure it was Johnny Cornflakes," I tried to convince them.

"I recognized his limp. I saw him under the street lamp. I know it was Johnny. Anyway," I added, "I'd certainly recognize that big, ugly shoe he drags along!"

"Yes, I'm sure they hurt Johnny. He was bent over and holding his stomach when he stood up."

"No, I have no idea where Johnny went. I haven't seen him all week."

After all the questions were asked and answered, I saw a pained look come across Paul's face.

"You know, Denise," he said, "it takes a brave man to do what Johnny did last Saturday night. He could have been killed. He must really care about you." I thought for a moment about the possibility that had never occurred to me.

Could Johnny Cornflakes really care about me? I had never said a kind word to Johnny. I had done nothing but insult the old man. How could he care about me? I wondered.

"Do you really think he cares about me?" I asked Paul.

"I don't know," Paul answered. "But he cared enough to try to protect you against a whole gang, didn't he?"

I took that question straight to my heart. It remained my constant companion for the following two weeks.

Why had Johnny risked his life in order to protect me? Could it be true? Could he actually care about me? I had never considered myself anything to Johnny but an occasional free lunch handed to him out the back door. Love? Johnny Cornflakes, capable of love?

That week I finally decided to unpack my dishes. Even though I longed to go back home, it looked like we would be staying in Chelsea for a while. As I placed the cups and saucers inside the kitchen cabinets, I thought about Johnny's heroic deed. And I began to wonder about the old man who kept a bottle of cheap wine by his side and who stumbled through the streets of the dirty city I was finally beginning to call "home."

Chapter 6

I worked hard during those next few weeks before Christmas. The children in the church basement day care had definitely caught the Christmas spirit. Everything seemed magical to them during the Christmas season. They loved the music, the lights, and the snow. When Paul dressed up in Santa garb and surprised us with a visit, each child sat on his lap and rattled off his or her Christmas wish list.

"What do you want for Christmas?" Paul asked Mitchell, a thin Spanish boy.

"I want a bicycle and a baseball bat," Mitchell answered before adding, "and I want my daddy to come see me."

Michelle's wish was similar. "I want my mommy to be well again and I want us to always have enough food to eat."

By the time little Rachel climbed upon Santa's red-velveted lap, I saw tears forming in Paul's eyes. "I want my mommy to get off drugs and come back home," the small black girl cried.

Christmastime brought rare smiles to the faces of the city's preschoolers. They decorated the halls of the day care with handmade reindeer and wreaths of green holly and red berries. The crayoned pictures on the walls told the stories of these young children. They showed dogs and cats, brothers and sisters, a mother and a grandmother, standing by a lopsided Christmas tree. Never in these

49

pictures did I see a father, nor did I ever see a brother older than sixteen. It seemed that young fathers and older brothers didn't stay long inside the family structures. Fragmented families were one of the many tragedies of inner-city life. Somehow, with little means, the women kept the families together and saved enough money to provide a meager Christmas for the children.

One afternoon, as I made my way to the post office in knee-high snow to mail a handful of Christmas cards, I caught sight of a stooped-over, white-haired man in a weathered navy suit.

"Johnny!" I called and raced through the snow to reach him. "Johnny, I just want to thank..." I cut my statement short when the old man turned around and gave me a puzzled stare.

"I'm sorry, sir. I thought you were someone else," I said as I turned away.

As I walked through the falling snow toward home, I began to wonder about this character that we called Johnny Cornflakes.

"Just who are you?" I asked aloud as I turned onto Shurtleff Street. "Where do you come from? Do you have a home? How did you end up in the streets of Chelsea?" For some unknown reason, I had the strange desire to know more about this man who had stuck out his neck (or rather, his stomach) on my behalf that Saturday night when I was frightened out of my wits.

At least I owed him a decent "thank you." Anyway, six concerned teenagers were daily searching the streets for him; everywhere they went, they carried the new shoe in their hands. At least if I could find him, they could give him his shoe.

That afternoon, I made a few visits around town. Surely someone in this city would know something about Johnny. But I couldn't find anyone who knew anything about him. He seemed to have no past, just appearing one day on the dirty streets of Chelsea. Late that night, as Timothy and I lay in bed listening to the planes and sirens of the city, a sudden thought hit me.

"Timothy," I said, sitting up in bed. "Johnny saved my life. He risked his life to save mine. We've got to do something about Johnny. We can't let him freeze to death out on the streets of Chelsea this winter. It wouldn't be the Christian thing to do."

"What do you have in mind?" Timothy asked.

"Well, we have that garage room downstairs. I mean we could clean out all the junk and make it into a room for Johnny. At least he could live there during the freezing winter months."

"That's not a bad idea, Denise. The garage is underground so it stays warm. It has a separate door that Johnny could use to go in and out. And we could repair that old toilet and shower that haven't been used for three or four decades. Might work."

With that affirmation, I put my plan into action. The next morning, I woke early and, with coffee in hand, I walked down the basement stairs to inspect the garage room that was to become Johnny's new home.

It would take a lot of work to make it into a decent bedroom, but for some strange reason, I was beginning to care a little something about the old man with the mysterious past. At the very least, I felt sorry for him. I imagined that garage room would soon become a castle to him.

"It'll be a lot of work," I told Timothy later that morning after I had inspected Johnny's new home. "But Johnny will be delighted. Can't you just see the expression on his face when we tell him about it?"

I spent that afternoon down in the garage room, cleaning, vacuuming, and scrubbing the old toilet and shower (which, with a few adjustments, checked out in workable condition).

Timothy and I, with the help of Jason and Paul, moved the guest room twin bed down the stairs to the garage room. With all the junk cleared out, the room began to take on tones of a real bedroom. "We just need some pictures on the wall and maybe a table and comfortable chair and a lamp," I told Paul. Paul and I scouted around the basement of the church and found the items Johnny needed for his new home.

"Let's use these sheets on the bed," I suggested, as I unwrapped the plastic from my new wedding gift sheets.

"I wonder when he last slept on clean sheets?!"

From my bedroom closet, I took Aunt Gertrude's quilt. I noted again the tiny handmade stitches and the scraps of cloth she had quilted into colorful designs. It was certainly a gift of love from Aunt Gertrude to me.

"Perhaps Johnny will be able to sense some of Aunt Gertrude's love as he sleeps beneath this quilt," I thought.

As Paul, Jason, Timothy, and I stood admiring the beautiful room, Timothy spoke up. "There's just one major problem, Denise. We don't have any idea where Johnny is. How do you suggest we find him to invite him to live in this room?"

I had already considered that problem. "We're going to search throughout all of Chelsea for Johnny," I told him. "And we're going to find him!"

Lisa and Jenny arrived at the parsonage first. Later that afternoon, Rick joined Jason, Paul, and me. While they searched the streets of Chelsea, I stayed home and made dozens of phone calls asking people to help us locate Johnny. Hours passed with no news of Johnny. I continued to telephone church members, hospitals, jails, shelters, and restaurant owners throughout Chelsea asking each one if they had seen Johnny recently.

I called Grady's Diner. "Grady," I asked. "Have you seen Johnny?"

"Nope," he shouted into the phone, as he dragged on his cigarette and called out orders to tired waitresses.

About ten o'clock that night, Timothy called off the search and the group came home.

They couldn't find Johnny. The temperature had already dropped below freezing. It was too cold to keep searching. They had just walked in the back door when I received a phone call from one of our elderly church members, the widow Mrs. Bena.

"Denise," the familiar voice said. "I have Johnny here in my parlor."

"You're kidding!" was all I could think to say. "Where did you find him? How did you convince him to come inside? Is he okay?"

"Oh, honey," she replied. "You're asking too many questions. When you telephoned to ask for my help, well, I just knew some of the right people to call to find him," she said. "I think I can keep him here long enough for you to drive over and pick him up. But you had better hurry, dear," she added. "He seems awfully restless."

Timothy and Paul hopped in the car and drove to Mrs. Bena's to claim Johnny Cornflakes. I made one last telephone call before Johnny came home.

"This is Denise George," I told the elderly woman who answered the phone. "May I please speak to Sam?"

"He's at a friend's house tonight," she told me. "But he'll be back in the morning. Can I have him call you?"

"Thank you, but I don't need to talk with him. Would you please just give him a message? It's very important that he receive it. Could you tell him to come to the parsonage tomorrow morning and bring the new shoe we've been keeping for Johnny Cornflakes? He'll know what I'm talking about."

"I'd be glad to. I'll tell him first thing in the morning," she said politely and hung up the phone.

I couldn't wait to see Johnny's reaction when he saw the finished room. And I also couldn't wait until our little group finally presented him with his new custom-made shoe.

When Timothy and Paul helped Johnny into the house, I noticed that the old man clutched a whiskey bottle to his chest.

"Johnny," I said, reaching for the bottle. "We've got a big surprise for you, but let's leave the liquor outside."

Johnny reeked with the stench of alcohol. I wondered if the smell would wash out of the new sheets and Aunt Gertrude's quilt. But it didn't matter. In my mind and heart, Johnny was quickly becoming one of the "least of these" that Jesus described in the Gospel of Matthew. And I was going to feed him, clothe him, and provide him with comfortable shelter. In fact I, single-handedly, was determined to change his life.

Just wait until the city of Chelsea sees Johnny Cornflakes when I'm finished with him, I thought.

Johnny hesitated when I took away his whiskey bottle. At first I didn't think he would let me take it. But I was determined that Johnny would leave his alcohol outside. The church parsonage was certainly no place for a bottle of whiskey. Anyway, when Johnny saw his new room, he'd sober up, straighten out his life, and give up all his bad habits. *Who knows*, I thought. *Johnny might become a respectable Chelsea resident.*

If my arm had been long enough I might have patted myself on the back for the miracle I was going to pull off. I felt proud of myself that day—too proud.

We helped Johnny down the stairs to his new room. But he had drunk too much whiskey to notice the clean sheets or the handmade quilt. We took off his worn shoes and tucked him into bed.

"He'll be so surprised when he wakes up in the morning," I said, misty-eyed. "I can hardly wait to see his reaction when the sun comes up and he discovers he has a home."

Early the next morning, I scrambled eggs and smeared toast with jelly. *Feed the hungry*. I poured a cup of hot coffee and a tall glass of orange juice and set them on the tray by the plate. *Give drink to the thirsty*. Then I carefully made my way down the basement stairs to the garage room.

"Johnny," I called, and tapped lightly on the door. I imagined that Johnny's poor head would be throbbing, so I had brewed the coffee extra strong for him.

"Johnny," I called again. Balancing the tray on one arm,

I turned the doorknob to his room. His room was pitch dark. I knew he was probably still asleep. I wondered if I should wake him for breakfast or just let him sleep.

He'll appreciate a hot breakfast, I thought, and I switched on the lamp. "Johnny?" I called to the bed with crumpled covers.

"Johnny!" I called again.

Johnny hadn't heard me because Johnny wasn't there.

I pulled back the covers to convince myself he wasn't lost somewhere in the new sheets. Putting the tray beside his bed, I looked in the closet, in the bathroom, and under the bed.

But Johnny was gone. I ran through the house trying to find him. As I bounded into the kitchen, trying to figure out what had happened to him, someone knocked at the back door.

"Johnny!" I exclaimed as I opened the door. "How did you lock yourself out of the..."

It wasn't Johnny. It was Sam who stood outside the door and gave me a puzzled look. "Were you expecting Johnny, Denise?" he asked as he stood outside waiting for me to invite him in.

"I thought you might be Johnny," I told him.

"But Grandma told me that Johnny was here with you. Look," he said as he held out the large box. "I got your message and I brought Johnny's new shoe."

"Well I've got bad news, Sam," I began. I felt the

frustration start to build inside me. "Johnny's gone. He must have left in the middle of the night or early this morning."

I remembered the whiskey bottle I had placed on the back porch. "Just a minute," I told Sam and walked to the corner of the porch and then returned to the kitchen. "And he must have taken his whiskey bottle with him," I said.

Chapter 7

I didn't have the heart to walk down the basement stairs to the garage room after Johnny disappeared. Lisa came over that day, made up the bed, turned out the lamp, and brought up the quilt and breakfast tray. I felt sorry for the old man, but something inside me loathed him for destroying my dreams of making him into a first-class, church-going citizen.

"Once a drunk, always a drunk," I muttered under my breath. Johnny had not even bothered to thank me for all the hard work I put into making the garage room a home for him. He could have at least had the decency to thank me. Maybe Johnny was hopeless after all. Just how could a person help "the least of these" when he didn't want to be helped, when he wouldn't cooperate with all the wonderful plans I had made for him?

The ring of the phone interrupted my thoughts.

"Hello. Yes, this is the parsonage. Yes, Timothy George is in the next room. Hold on a moment, and I'll get him." As Timothy listened to the caller, I noticed that his face took on a serious expression.

"Yes, Johnny was here last night. No, he wasn't here when we woke up this morning. Oh, I'm sorry to hear that. Frozen to death? Yes, I guess I can come down and identify the body."

Identify the body?! The old man I had been hating for the last few minutes was dead? Frozen to death? Hadn't Timothy just said those words? When Timothy hung up the telephone, I had an explosion of questions to ask him.

"Timothy, is Johnny dead?"

"I'm afraid so, Denise," Timothy whispered, shocked himself at the tragic news.

"Who called you?"

"The county morgue," he answered.

"Well," I continued, "why did they call you?"

"They said they wanted to have one of the city's clergymen identify the body," he stated. Timothy zipped up his heaviest jacket and left. I heard the crunch of frozen rain and snow as he stepped down onto the sidewalk. *Why? Why didn't Johnny stay in his nice warm bed last night?* I asked myself again and again. *Why did he venture out into the freezing temperature and deep snow when he could have been warm inside our home?*

"The crazy old drunk," I heard myself shout. I reached for Aunt Gertrude's quilt, wrapped myself deep within its tiny stitches and fluffy stuffing, sat down on the couch, and cried. That's when I remembered why I cared so much for the old man who cared so little about life and who reeked of alcohol. I remembered the night he stood beneath my bedroom window and risked his life to protect me from the gang of youths with their crowbars and their evil intentions. Johnny took a hard blow to the stomach for me. Why wouldn't he let me repay him with a warm bed and a good breakfast?

It was a dark day for me. I waited on the couch and thought back on the tragedy of Johnny's life and yearned for Timothy's return.

I put on a pot of fresh coffee for Timothy as I continued to wait for him to come home. The wind had picked up since morning. I expected rain or sleet or more snow any moment. I hoped Timothy would come home before the storm started. A tree branch scratched against the living room window. We had one small tree in our fenced yard. I worried that the wind would be strong enough to uproot it.

"What are they going to do with Johnny's body?" I asked my husband when he walked in the door. "What kind of funeral will he have?" I continued with my questions and poured the coffee.

"Denise, wait a minute. Sit down. I have something to tell you." I sat down and stared into Timothy's face.

"It wasn't Johnny, Denise," he said. "The frozen body wasn't Johnny. No one knows who the old man is, but it isn't Johnny."

It took several seconds for me to digest his words.

"You mean Johnny Cornflakes is still alive somewhere? He hasn't frozen to death?" My mouth flew open and my reddened eyes showed my bewilderment. I felt a surge of happiness that I hadn't felt for a long time. I wanted to jump up and down in excitement like a little girl presented with a new Barbie doll. Johnny was alive after all! I could hardly believe the good news. I instinctively glanced at the fireplace mantle and at the large box Sam had brought over earlier that morning—the box that held Johnny's new shoe.

Chapter 8

Well, wherever Johnny is," Timothy told me, "I hope he will find some shelter. The wind is blowing hard, and it looks like we're going to have a whopper of a snowstorm."

The day grew darker and an ominous cloud covered the city as the wind picked up and blew discarded trash across town. I was the first one who heard the fire truck siren scream down the hill from our house, and I opened the front door to see what was happening. I immediately smelled smoke.

"I'll bet another apartment building or something is on fire," I told Timothy, who had come to the front door to investigate.

A few minutes later, Jason ran by our house. "The tire factory's on fire," he yelled as he ran down the hill toward the factory. Jason's face was flushed and his hands were knotted into fists. "There's lots of people who won't have jobs tomorrow if that factory burns down," he yelled.

Soon the smell of burning rubber filled the air. It was a strong, stifling smell that was picked up and carried by the unusually swift wind. We soon learned that the fire was quickly spreading into other parts of our city.

I turned on the small black and white television to see if I could find out more about the fire. Yes, it was spreading. The tire factory had been razed and the fire had leaped onto several nearby apartment buildings.

It seemed the Chelsea firefighters couldn't bring the flames under control.

I worried that my family back in Georgia would hear the news and panic. I picked up the telephone and called my parents—long-distance calls were expensive and I rarely made them.

"Daddy," I said. "There's a fire in our city, and it seems to be spreading by the wind. Don't worry about us if you see the story on the news. If it spreads much more, we will leave the city. We'll call you and let you know we're okay."

The fire raged all afternoon. The intense wind picked up the flames and carried them from one wooden apartment building to the next. Businesses, restaurants, and public city buildings fell one by one into the grasp of the flames. Oil-burning furnaces exploded time and time again as the flames swallowed up old buildings.

Exhausted Chelsea firefighters trudged through the snow and worked until midnight trying to control the fire that threatened to ravage the entire city. Other cities had sent their own fire trucks and firefighters to help put out the Chelsea fire. But the fire seemed to have a mind of its own. It leaped at random from building to building, and sent residents scurrying out into the icy streets clutching only their most treasured possessions. They had no time to pack their belongings or dress their children.

The flames were too swift, too sudden. I watched with grief and fear from my bedroom window as the flames shot up into the midnight sky. Fiery fingers of bright yellow, orange, and red reached up above the skyline. Exploding furnaces sounded like rapid gunfire. People crowded the streets, running in insane directions, trying to escape the destruction of the city.

About 1:00 A.M. I asked a practical question. "Do you think we need to pack our things, Timothy? Do you think the fire will reach this part of the city?"

"I doubt it," Timothy responded. "But it might be a good idea to keep watch at the window and see where it's headed."

At 2:15 A.M. someone knocked on our front door. When Timothy opened the door, a soot-smeared face appeared. Out of breath, the frustrated firefighter told us to start packing.

"We're going to evacuate Bellingham Street next," he shouted. "We've already evacuated Shurtleff Street. Better pack what you can carry and get ready to leave."

"What's going on out there?" Timothy asked him. "What can we do to help?"

"We're just asking the citizens to leave the city as quickly as possible," the fireman said. "We can't get this fire under control. We've already lost three fire trucks to the flames. We'll be battling the flames in front of us, and the wind will whip the flames up behind us. We can't move the fire trucks fast enough to keep them from catching fire."

Again I picked up the telephone and made a long-distance call to my parents.

"Daddy," I began. "We're going to evacuate our house in a little while. The fire has changed directions again and is coming into this part of the city."

"We've been watching the news reports about the fire," Daddy told me. "Are you okay?"

"We're fine, Daddy. But please don't worry about us if you try to call and the telephone lines are down. We'll be okay."

"Your mother and I are praying for you, and we have our whole church praying too. Please call us and let us know how…"

The phone went dead. I heard Timothy's frantic call coming from outside the house.

"Denise! Come help me! Turn on the outside water faucet!" he shouted.

I ran out into the front yard. Sparks of fire and embers were landing on the roof. Timothy had the garden hose in his hands, pointing it at the roof. "Turn on the water!" Timothy called, expecting a blast of cold water. But nothing happened.

"Turn on the water!" Timothy called again.

"I did! I turned it on!" I yelled back.

"The hose is frozen up!" he cried. "With all the sparks, the roof will go up in flames!" I ran to Timothy. The air was thick with smoke. Apartment buildings had already caught fire on Shurtleff Street. We received another urgent message from a running firefighter. "Evacuate! Evacuate! Leave this area immediately!"

I ran into the house and grabbed my coat. What did I want to save? My eyes searched the living room—there was no time to hesitate. Did I want to save the family photos, the new typewriter, the quilt, the silver tea service? I didn't know. I couldn't make up my mind and certainly couldn't carry it all. Again I heard the firefighter order us to evacuate.

"Hurry up, Denise!" Timothy shouted.

For some reason, the large box on the fireplace mantle caught my eye. In a split second, I thought about how much Johnny needed that shoe and how much our little group of teenagers had sacrificed and worked to earn enough money to buy the shoe. I surely didn't want to be the one to have to tell them that Johnny's new shoe had burned up in the fire. I made my way quickly to the mantle and grabbed the shoebox. Planting it securely under my arm, I stopped and took one last look back at the silver tea service, my most prized possession. Then with the box under my arm, I made a wild dash for the front door. Within minutes, firefighters took over Bellingham Street, soaking everything in sight with their huge water hoses and fighting the flames that still threatened to consume the whole city.

Timothy and I and the other residents of Chelsea trudged quickly through the crowded, smoke-filled streets in a desperate attempt to leave the burning city. We stopped only to help mothers with their children and to carry babies and small pets.

When we finally stood safely on the outskirts of Chelsea, I stopped and checked for the parcel I had stashed under my arm. To my relief, it was still there. Timothy and I had somehow escaped the roaring flames with our lives—and with Johnny's $113.92 shoe.

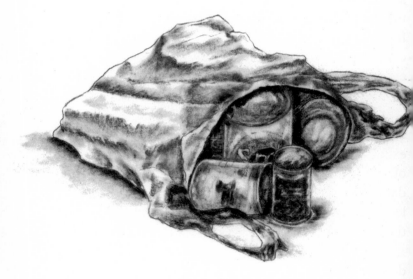

Chapter 9

*I*f I live to be a hundred years old, I will never forget the way Chelsea sounded, looked, and smelled when the sun finally came up. Sometime in the early hours of the morning, the winds calmed down and the firefighters finally contained the flames. We walked back into the city, coughing through the thick black smoke that covered everything like a heavy, woolen blanket. The snow on the ground had been partially melted and blackened by soot.

At least half of Chelsea had been destroyed. Great hulls of burned fire trucks lined the streets. Firefighters sat exhausted on the curbs, too tired to get up. Only the shells of apartments and businesses surrounded us. The residents with their children and neighbors stood outside the leveled buildings and cried loudly. No one had expected the fire to do so much damage.

With the exception of crying women and children, a deathly silence covered the city.

"Had the wind not been so swift," one man told us, "the fire wouldn't have been so unpredictable and widespread."

"I heard that some gang members purposely started the fire in the tire factory," another Chelsea resident told us.

"Thank God no one died in that awful fire," Mrs. Bena told us on the street outside her damaged home. "Plenty of people were hurt," she continued, "but thank God no one died."

"Let's check the church and parsonage," Timothy said as we made our way through the bevy of broken-hearted people to Shurtleff Street. I expected to see the old rock church with its beautiful stained glass windows and tall steeple lying in ruins. I braced myself to see what was left of our house.

When we arrived at Bellingham Street, Lisa, Jenny, Rick, Sam, Jason, and Paul met us there. "The church and the parsonage are still standing," they told us to our sudden relief. "There was some damage to the roof, but other than that, they're in good shape."

Sure enough, even through the smoke and cinders that filled the air, the untouched stained glass windows of the church caught a ray of sunshine and sparkled a welcome to us.

"It's a miracle," I said. "A miracle."

The cries of Chelsea's people lasted all day. Most had lost everything they owned, including decorated Christmas trees and hard-earned Christmas gifts beneath those trees. It took a full week before the smoke cleared. Since our church proved to be the only big building still standing in Chelsea, we opened the doors to the people. They came in droves, sleeping on blankets and cots, eating what little food we could find in the church kitchen. Within days, however, great vats of food began to arrive. I put on an old pair of Timothy's overalls and a pair of Lisa's work boots. Our little group of teenagers worked beside us twenty hours a day. We stacked canned foods and distributed fresh produce to all who could carry it.

Jenny, Lisa, and Rick took charge of the church kitchen, opening the doors to a team of volunteers who offered to cook and serve food to the community's cold and homeless.

Sam and Paul organized the clothes closet. Donations of clothing came in from around the world, even from as far away as Australia. Daily we sorted through pounds and pounds of new and second-hand clothing, dividing the clothes by sizes and helping Chelsea's victims find enough to wear.

Streams of people passed through the church's open doors. They sought shelter, warmth, counseling, financial help, clothes, and food. We had never worked harder or longer. The whole city seemed to fit into the category of "the least of these."

By the week before Christmas, the city had settled down somewhat. Most families had traveled to the homes of relatives or had moved to other parts of the state. We were glad to learn that Mrs. Bena decided to stay in Chelsea. Few people needed our help anymore as they ventured out to new areas, new jobs, and new futures. Our supply of food and clothes had all been given to the needy.

By Friday night, Christmas Eve, our exhausted group of teenagers sat in the basement of the church in the same metal folding chairs, listened to the sound of the guitar, and ate potato chips. After a brief Bible study, we prayed together and bundled up to go home. It didn't seem much like Christmas Eve. We were exhausted, and too much sadness surrounded us. We missed friends who had moved away and wondered if Chelsea would ever be rebuilt.

"You know, we've been able to help a lot of people over the last two weeks," Sam said.

We nodded our heads in agreement. It had been a rewarding experience, but a devastating one, too.

"But," Sam continued, "there's still one person left to help."

We turned to look at one another. Had we left someone out? Was there still a family who needed our help? Who needed clothes or food?

"Who are you talking about?" Lisa asked.

Softly, Sam spoke the name of a person we had not thought about since the fire. We had been so busy, worked such long hours, and offered help to so many of Chelsea's residents that we had forgotten the one person we most wanted to help: Johnny Cornflakes.

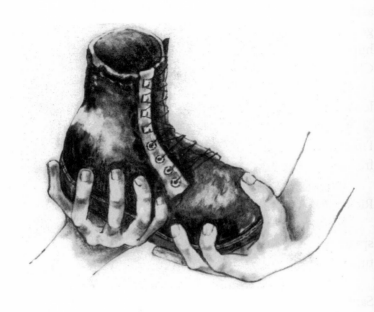

Chapter 10

*B*efore we left the church that Christmas Eve night, I asked a question. "Well, what shall we do?" I asked. "We've got to find Johnny before we can help him. We've not seen him since the fire. We don't even know if he is still living in Chelsea, or even still alive."

Lisa spoke first. "I think we should go out tonight and look for him."

But Jenny disagreed. "I don't know about you guys, but I'm exhausted. The temperatures are dropping and it's already freezing outside. It's much too cold to start searching tonight."

"We could wait till morning and then look for him," Rick spoke up.

"But tomorrow is Christmas Day. And we've planned to spend the day delivering Christmas dinners. We won't have time to search for Johnny," offered Jason.

"I'll go along with whatever the rest of you decide," said Sam. "But I vote for finding Johnny tonight."

For the next few minutes, we sat still and thought about our options. Jenny was right. It was extremely cold outside, too cold and snowy to be out running around the city. But Christmas Day would be too busy to search for Johnny.

"We could always wait until after the holidays and then look for him," Jason said.

That settled it. We decided to wait until the first of the new year and then resume our search for Johnny Cornflakes.

We put on coats, hats, scarves, and gloves, locked the front door of the church, and each of us headed in a different direction for home.

Timothy unlocked the back door of the parsonage, but before we could go inside, I stopped him.

"Timothy," I asked. "Do you really want to wait another week or so to give Johnny his new shoe? I mean, wouldn't it be great if we could give him the shoe for Christmas?"

"But Denise, we agreed to..."

"I know we agreed to wait," I acknowledged. "But do you think you and I could go out and just look a few places where he might be? We could look for about an hour. If we don't find him we can give up and come home."

"You love the old man, don't you?" Timothy grinned.

"No, Timothy, of course I don't love Johnny. I just feel sorry for him. And I don't want the county morgue calling us again to come identify his frozen body!"

"Okay," Timothy agreed, "but don't get your hopes up. Johnny could be hundreds of miles away from Chelsea by now."

"Let me call Grady," I told Timothy as I walked into the kitchen and picked up the phone.

"What?!" Grady shouted into the mouthpiece.

It was his own unique way of saying "hello."

"Grady, have you seen Johnny hanging around the diner?"

"Don't bother me about Johnny!" he barked. "I've got

80

enough to do right now without worrying about that old man! Anyway, I ain't seen him."

Click. The phone went down hard.

"Grady hasn't seen him," I told Timothy as I lifted the large shoebox off the fireplace mantle and pushed it up under my arm. Dirt and smoky soot now covered the once white box, but the shoe inside was intact and clean. Timothy reached for the flashlight.

This time I led the search. I walked as fast as I could so we could cover as much territory as possible before our one-hour time limit ended.

Unlike the last few searches, this time I, too, crawled under apartment porches, checked out some local restaurant alleys, searched the city's trash bins, and walked the dirty, wet streets calling his name.

We combed the city for forty-five minutes without a clue about the whereabouts of Johnny Cornflakes.

"Denise, I think this is hopeless," Timothy finally said.

The words choked in my throat. "I guess you're right, Timothy, but let's look just one more place," I begged. "If we don't find him at Grady's Diner, then we'll go home."

"You said Grady hadn't seen him," Timothy reminded me. But it was my last hope. Even though Grady had told me Johnny wasn't there, I was just stubborn enough to want to check it out myself.

Most of Chelsea's restaurants had been ravaged by fire. Grady's Diner, however, had been untouched by the blaze.

I imagined Grady standing by the large dirty grill, where he always stood. He'd probably opened his smoke-filled restaurant to serve up some Christmas Eve dinners to hungry folks still left in Chelsea. I didn't care much for the tough old bird. But however rough he was, somewhere buried deep inside Grady's hairy tattooed chest, I recognized my beloved grandmother's heart—a heart of gold that genuinely loved and cared for the down-and-outers of society, the little barefoot girls of the world, and the old town drunks.

We shivered from the cold. Muddy water soaked our gloves and shoes. Sleet began to pelt the desolate city as we walked through dirty piles of snow to the back door of Grady's Diner.

"It will be a miracle if we find Johnny here," I told Timothy. "But I don't know where else to look for him."

The alley was dark, too dark to see anything. We shined our flashlight around the diner's back door entrance and I prepared myself to be disappointed. Maybe it just wasn't meant for us to find Johnny, I thought.

The alley was empty...except for...could it be?

"Timothy, shine the flashlight at the corner of the building!" I shouted. And there, caught in the narrow beam of the flashlight was a...shoe! Yes!

"Look Timothy!" I screamed.

A huge dirty old shoe with a large gaping hole was all I saw, but I knew that behind that building's corner lay the old man we had painstakingly searched for. The shoe held a valued prize—a twisted mass of unsocked foot that belonged to the one and only Johnny Cornflakes.

"I'd know that shoe anywhere," I told Timothy. "That's Johnny's foot!"

We ran around the corner and our eyes immediately landed on the beautiful figure of Johnny—sprawled out drunk in the alley, soaking wet, and covered with mud.

"Johnny!" I shouted. "We found you!"

I couldn't believe we had actually found the old man. I knelt down close to him to see if he was still alive. Yes, he was still breathing.

"Johnny," I pleaded, "tell me you're okay! Are you okay, Johnny?"

He opened his eyes, blinked a few times, and then slowly raised one hand. "Yep," he whispered. "I'm okay. Just cold. And tired."

With that good word from him, I could hardly wait to tell him the good news. "Johnny, we've got a gift—a Christmas gift—for you. It's from the Bible study group at the church."

Kneeling down beside the old man who had spent a lifetime sprawled out in one alley or another, Timothy gently pulled Johnny's worthless foot from his weathered shoe. I opened the box under my arm and unwrapped the new shoe.

"Look, Johnny," I smiled. "Look what the Bible study group bought for you."

Timothy and I together tenderly placed Johnny's deformed foot into the new shoe. It was a perfect fit. As I tied the long shoestrings, the back door of the diner swung open.

Grady, himself, came out into the alley, looked around the dark corner, and squinted his eyes. In his huge hands, he carried a plastic bag full of food scraps.

"Johnny? Is that you out there?" Grady called. "Where've you been, old man?" He seemed as glad to see Johnny as we were. Surely the heart within Grady beat as happily as our hearts. Grady flipped a switch on the outside wall and a dim yellow bug light interrupted the darkness.

"Here's something to eat, old man. And get out of the snow, Johnny! You'll freeze to death." Then he added with a deep rough voice and a rare grin, "And Merry Christmas, Johnny. Merry Christmas to you." As he tossed the bag of food over to Johnny, Grady hesitated. In the low glow of the yellow bulb, he saw me sitting beside Johnny. He looked me square in the face and made a statement that made my heart skip a beat—maybe two.

"Here, lady," he said. "There's probably enough for you in there, too!"

As he shut the back door, I caught my yellowed reflection in the glass. I was shocked by what he had said and by what I now saw.

There I was, kneeling in the alley beside the town drunk, my hair wet and disheveled, my clothes covered with mud and snow. I had never been so humiliated in my life. How dare he! Grady had certainly misjudged me. He couldn't see beneath the layers of city dirt to know who I really was. No one had ever spoken to me like that. An appalling thought came to mind: he thinks I'm a bag lady!

I looked again at Johnny, who now sat up and stared at his new shoe. Tears slid down his cheeks and dropped off his stubbly chin. Overwhelmed with gratitude, he couldn't speak. Instead, he turned his entire body toward me and gazed at my face with those same bloodshot eyes and then opened his food-encrusted, toothless mouth, and smiled. The smell of body odor and old alcohol met my nose, but for some reason I wasn't repelled by it. My hand no longer reached out to cover my face; instead, it reached out and touched Johnny's face. And feeling an unexpected tenderness for him, I smiled back.

"Forgive me, Johnny," was all I could say as I knelt in the snow beneath the yellow bulb. Feeling the warmth and softness of his face, I added, "Perhaps I have misjudged you, too."

A long silence prevailed before Timothy broke the silence. "Guess what?" he said, looking at his watch. "It's 12:01 A.M. It's Christmas Day!"

"Merry Christmas, Johnny," I said softly, still looking into Johnny's deep eyes.

"Merry Christmas to you," Johnny answered. "And thank you," he added. "Thank you for everything."

In the predawn hours of Christmas morning, in a dark alley in Chelsea, Massachusetts, Johnny Cornflakes helped me learn a profound lesson about life. In God's eyes, we are all precious and valuable, every person, every "least of these"—whether we are a shaggy-haired teenager, a spoiled pastor's wife, or an old town drunk with a brand-new $113.92 shoe.

Chapter 11

*S*omehow, in those early hours of Christmas morning, we managed to convince Johnny to come home with us. Timothy slipped off his gloves and put them on Johnny's rough, red hands. When we helped him to his feet, Johnny instinctively picked up the old weathered shoe with the gaping hole in the toe. I guess after so many years it had become a part of him.

The three of us slowly walked home. Each time we passed beneath a street light, Johnny stopped, held up his foot, and looked at his new shoe. Perhaps he was trying to convince himself he wasn't dreaming.

Once home, we ate a hearty plate of scrambled eggs and drank several mugs of hot chocolate. Exhausted from the search, Timothy and I tucked Johnny into his bed in the garage room, covered him with Aunt Gertrude's quilt, and headed upstairs for our own bed.

We slept until the late morning hours of Christmas Day. When we finally woke up, we made quick telephone calls to Lisa, Jenny, Rick, Sam, Jason, and Paul.

"You'll never guess who we found last night at Grady's Diner," we told them happily. "Yes, Johnny Cornflakes!" I said. "And he loves his new shoe. It was a perfect fit."

I passed the phone to Timothy. "He's still downstairs asleep," he said.

"Yes, you can come over and we'll wake him and

surprise him together."

One by one the teenagers gathered in our kitchen. I scrambled more eggs and fed each hungry person. After we passed the coffeepot around once more, we decided it was time to wake Johnny.

Together, excitedly, we tiptoed downstairs and knocked lightly on his bedroom door. I put my ear to the door, expecting to hear him still loudly snoring.

But I heard nothing.

Timothy quietly opened the door, and I turned on a soft light in his room.

But Johnny was gone.

Unlike before, this time he had neatly folded back the sheets and had smoothed the quilt. On top of the table by his bed, he had left us a "gift"—to him, a precious gift. Leaving his old shoe was Johnny's unique way of saying thank you and Merry Christmas. Yes, we had experienced a very unexpected Christmas.

Before long, Timothy's graduation day came. We packed what few belongings we had left, walked out the back door of the parsonage, and said some tearful good-byes to our friends. We were heading South again, to a bluegrass Kentucky town where Timothy would teach church history. We left in the same old green Plymouth Satellite that we had driven into Chelsea years before.

Before we left, however, I ran back into the parsonage. In my hands I held the quilt, so lovingly stitched by Aunt

Gertrude. I decided to leave the quilt in the garage room that day. I thought maybe, just maybe, the new residents might let Johnny come back, if he ever wanted to live there again.

Epilogue

*I*t was a decade later before Timothy and I returned to visit Chelsea. We arrived early on a Sunday morning. The large stained glass windows still reflected the rising sun and sparkled a familiar welcome to us.

We noticed that Chelsea had rebuilt since the fire. New apartment buildings mingled with the old buildings still scorched by fire and smoke. We wondered if we would see anyone we had known during our "Chelsea days." As we sat in the still, quiet sanctuary of the huge old church, we silently reflected on the years of hard work and hard prayer we had invested into the lives of Chelsea's people.

Had our work mattered at all? Were the Bible study youth still involved in the church? Was Mrs. Bena still living in Chelsea and baking sugar cookies?

And what about Johnny Cornflakes? Was he still alive?

After thirty minutes or so of quiet reflection, people began to fill the old sanctuary. Young couples holding hands, families with children of all ages, old folks walking on canes, and teenagers coming in groups turned the wintery silence of the empty sanctuary into a blooming, active springtime.

Folks hugged, smiled, greeted each other, and complimented new lacy dresses worn by little girls. The church had definitely grown, its spirit sweet with Christian fellowship. But all the faces around us were new ones.

Timothy's eyes met mine and we both thought the same thought. Our Bible study "kids" could be scattered all over the world by now.

The century-old organ groaned some familiar hymn, the pastor made a few announcements, and everyone quieted down so the worship service could begin. Just then, I felt a light tap on my shoulder. I turned around to see Lisa, Jenny, Rick, Sam, Jason, and Paul beaming on the pew behind us! We created quite a commotion during the next few minutes. Sitting with the now grown "teenagers" were spouses and small children and at least one newborn baby. In fact, all together they filled up two long pews!

I was startled right down to my toes by the next sight I saw. An old man limped up to the pulpit and bowed his head. I didn't recognize him at first. His hair was cut and combed. His fingernails were clean and trimmed. While not the very latest style, his dark suit was neat and pressed. And his shoes—my eyes instinctively lowered to his shoes—his shoes were black, polished, and shiny. And they matched!

As I listened to the heartfelt, humble prayer spill from the old man's lips, it suddenly dawned on me. This man, this well-mannered old man was the one and only Johnny Cornflakes! In bewilderment, I turned and glanced at Lisa, who sat directly behind me. She looked straight at me, a smile formed on her lips, and she nodded her head as if to say, *Yes, Denise, it's Johnny! Can you hardly believe it?*

Needless to say, after the worship service, a great time of reunion followed. All the Bible study "teens" had stayed in Chelsea, had raised up families, and had continued to work together to build the church. They were now Chelsea's leading citizens and the ones teaching the Friday night coffee house Bible study for Chelsea's new batch of the "least of these" teens. Under the influence of Mrs. Bena and the Bible study group, Johnny had joined the grand old church built from hand-cut rock and laid down his liquor bottle forever.

I smiled, knowing that wherever Timothy and I moved, whatever prosperous southern town we settled in, I would never forget Chelsea, that group of troubled teenagers, or Johnny Cornflakes.